ACKNOWLEDGEMENT

In as much as i will like to take the credit for this book,I will like to acknowledge people's opinion,comments and contributions

All thanks to God for the ability to put this down
I could like to give thanks to my family and friends for inspiring this book. For your support..
Much love

TABLE OF CONTENTS

INTRODUCTION

We are God's masterpiece.He created us in his own image and likeness. He gave us abundantly something dear to our hearts which is "Ourselves" am nothing without and you are both without me
He gave us the union of marriage as a blessing to love and to cherish,nurture and love
Marriage is a union made in heaven which is why they said whosoever found a wife found blessing

This book will redirect your mind to a marriage made by God not created out of mere social obligations
Love and cherish your partner because that is Gods rules

This book will help you understand the concept of marriage and how to live up to it

I hereby recommend this easily readable book for youths and Adults who wants to make their marriage a happy place.

MARRIAGE

Marriage [v. t.]: The act of marrying, or the state of being married; legal union of a man and a woman for life, as husband and wife; wedlock; matrimony.

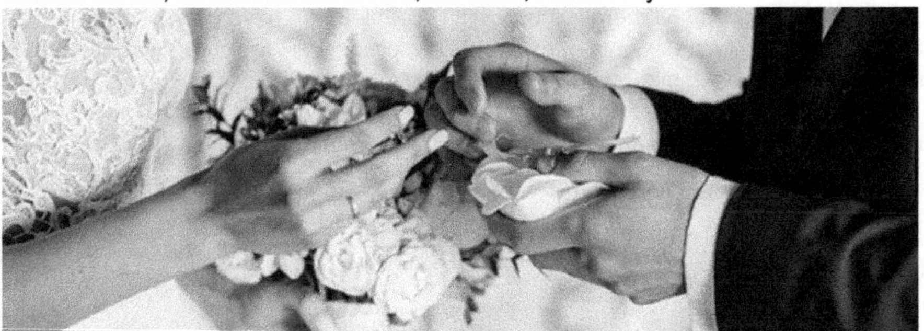

Marriage isn't a child play. We don't just marry for trials and error, we don't marry to check if the person is good in bed then run out when your expectations are not met. Marriage should not be a contract or a signed agreement with rules and regulations

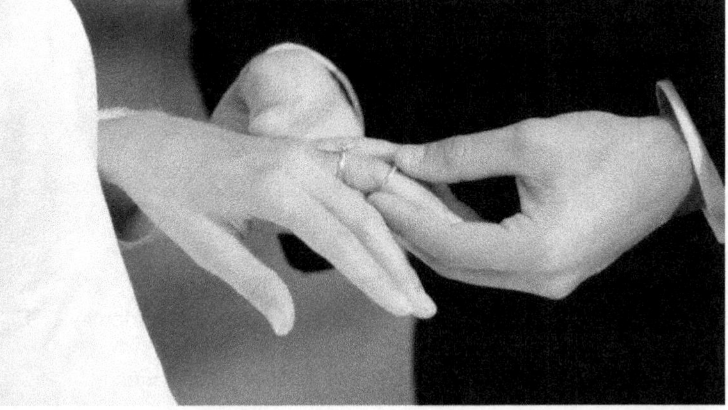

Marriage consists of two matured minds ready to nurture, tolerate and understand each other Marriage isn't a bed of roses and petals, marriage is not always gold and silver, marriage is something difficult and overwhelming. Marriage sometimes comes with pains, sacrifices

Marriage is always a testing ground for people. Those who fail in marriage cannot claim total success in any other areas of life. Marriage is always a turning point in every person's life. You can never rightly assess anybody until that person has been subjected to the trying fires of marriage predicaments. There is bound to be trials and adversities in marital relationships . Life is full of ups and downs. Engagement, wedding, honeymoon and romance quickly give way to challenges that make marriage, sometimes it seems very undesirable. When these trials and adversities like childlessness and sickness intrude into your marriage, use the greatest conquering weapon, "Patience" to overcome. Abraham and Sarah, Hannah and Ruth, David and Isaac are living examples. Today, there are very many couples who have been blessed with babies and money after many years of severe trials and childlessness. Prayerfully and patiently wait upon God. Do not blame each other nor regret ever getting married to one another because of severe trials. Couples who love each other will rather be knitted together in times of adverse trials. Unfortunately some couples allow such situations to break them and scatter them.
Dear Sister,

It is important to build up your spiritual Life.
Very important.
Beauty is the least strength of a Woman.
After 1,2 pregnancies and some kids, and some years, that chest that is making you feel on top can change its slope, that figure 8 shape can change alignment.
MAKE UP your Spiritual life, not just your Face.
So that you can see and hear beyond the limited capacity of your physical eyes and ears.
Some men are good now, but in 5 years time, they'll become something else.
And then work on your CHARACTER.
So that you will not be hard to want, and so that your Marriage will LAST..
Be calming down, let God lead you, not the Man's current bank account.
Does he have a car isn't the question..
Where he works isn't the question.
How much he earns isn't even the question.
The question is, "IS HE THE ONE?"
If he is not, every other thing is irrelevant.
If he is, every other thing is irrelevant.
Don't hook yourself to the Brother that is AVAILABLE, learn how to prepare/wait for/identify THE ONE......
The "AVAILABLE BROTHER" syndrome has landed many Sisters in Wrong Marriages.
May God arrest your Heart.
May you fall in love with Him, more than you are in Love with any Man.
May you not Marry a BRIDE DOOM, but rather, Marry a BRIDE GROOM.
You will MARRY and ENJOY, not MARRY and ENDURE.
BIG SECRETS IN MARRIAGE!
"Marriage Isn't About Your Happiness, Or Getting All Your Needs Met Through Another Person. Practicing self-denial & self-sacrifice, patience, understanding, & forgiveness are the fundamentals of a great marriage.
If you want to be the center of the universe, then there's a much Better chance of that happening if you stay single"~ "Love is patient, love is kind. It does not envy, or boast..." -1 Cor 13

MARRIAGE AND HAPPINESS
Marriage will not make you complete or happy & neither will it solve your loneliness. If you are not complete, happy & satisfied in your singleness, you will not suddenly become happy, complete & satisfied in married. Remember a person can be lonely in a crowd. Regardless of how loving your spouse is, he/she is unable to make you happy or satisfied if you don't want to or if you don't know how to. Love yourself & be comfortable in your skin. Be satisfied with yourself & be complete alone. Value yourself, celebrate singleness in the lord & be happy on

your own; and make a decision to remain the same in marriage regardless of what your spouse does or doesn't do. Happiness in a personal decision & satisfaction is the state of the mind. Anyone who enters into marriage unsatisfied & expecting to get filled by marriage is bound to experience perpetual emptiness throughout marriage. It's only happy singles that live happily ever after.

Secret 1
Everyone you marry has a weakness. Only God does not have a weakness. So if you focus on your spouse's weakness you can't get the best out of his strength.
People need to know that there is no perfect person outside,we all have weaknesses and that weaknesses made us who we are today. in marriages if you're with a perfect person or someone who claims to be perfect the marriage is likely going to have lots of issues because that's perfect Person will also want to change the other person to act and Behave the same way he or she does at some point this could get so frustrating for both partners. In marriage you need to acknowledge the strengths and weaknesses of our partners. We are required to learn and accommodate Others

FACTORS THAT EFFECT YOUR MARRIAGE

Your upbringing for cause you problems in your marriage

Sometime ago, I heard the story of a newly wedded couple. They were still in their honeymoon. So, one day they were eating together and the wife took meat and ate. The thing didn't sit well with the man and he cautioned her.
The wife was like what, because of meat? And that was how the problem started from their honeymoon.
The problem wasn't because she took the meat from the plate, no. The problem was because she took the meat when they had not finished eating.
This story brings me to my subject matter; upbringing. Whether you believe it or not, your upbringing can affect your relationship either positively or negatively.
Just like the couple above, there are homes where you don't dare touch your meat, even bones, until you are done with your food and there are homes even before they touch food, they've already sampled one or two meats depending on their buoyancy.
We all are raised uniquely and differently and it's very important you discuss your upbringing with whomever you are in a relationship with.
There are guys who their father never for once mentioned "I love you" to them nor receive love from their fathers. Today, they're finding it hard to give love.
The same thing with some ladies. Their father never told them how much they loved them. Today, they're vulnerable. Just one single "I love you" from a guy, they will fall.
Dear parents, learn to tell your children how much you love them. Done assume they know. Verbalize it.

Most of the views we hold about men and women today came from our upbringing, what our parents taught us, how our parents treated each other.
Just this afternoon, I read a post from a guy who his father taught that he should never see the wife he's going to marry as part of the family, that she's a stranger, not his relative nor blood. You can imagine the kind of things that this woman will pass through in the hand of this guy because of what he had taught him.
A guy that watches his father beat his mum for every single mistake, unless he knows better, he will beat his wife too. The same goes to a lady that watches her mother insults and disrespects her husband.
In conclusion, discuss your upbringing with your prospective partner. What did his parents teach him about women? Women are commodity and object of sexual satisfaction? How was he raised? What are the things his mother taught her about men? Men are scum? Are men the same? Men are cheats? What is their relationship with their parents like? Which of them do they flow well with and why? Discuss your upbringing.
I had a friend who broke up with her boyfriend of 2 years because the guy said she wasn't washing his clothes, My question is, is it right for a girl to make it her duty to wash her boyfriend's clothes when they're not married yet? To some people this practice is regarded as a wife duty not girlfriend while to some it's normal to do Laundry for their partner
In her case she was against the idea of doing laundry for her boyfriend because their are not married yet but the guy having been brought up in a culture that makes the girls do laundry for their boyfriend sees not sense in her excuses rather he sees it as being lazy and unreasonable, they both couldn't sort the problem due to their different upbringing, the girl saw it has enslavement while the guy saw it as her duty..this is very it is very important to ask questions and get to know each other well

Secret 2
Everyone has a dark history. No one is an angel. When you get married or you want to get married stop digging into someone's past. What matters most is the present life of your partner. Old things have passed away. Forgive and forget. Focus on the present and the future.

Nobody fell down from the skies he or she had a life before you both met in some cases it is advisable to let your past be in your past some people might advise not to share your past relationship experience with your partner the reason is some people might not be able to handle the past some people might even judge you for your past but I need people to understand that there is no future without a past that does not mean you should live in your past let go of your past and begin to live in your present
The worst case scenario is judging someone based on their past experience that they told you about this is a major turn off please don't do it because such person won't want to confide in you the next time to avoid being used as a topic

Secret 3
Every marriage has its own challenges. Marriage is not a bed of roses. Every good marriage has gone through its own test of blazing fire. True love proves in times of challenges. Fight for

your marriage. Make up your mind to stay with your spouse in times of need. Remember the vow For better for worse. In sickness and in health be there.challenges is a part of life,part of marriage in fact a part of human existence

Challenges can come in any form it could be family crisis,financial difficulties, health problem etc
If we all run away from our problems or leave our marriages because it got rocky then you are not even ready to stay married because the problems and challenges you are running from do not only exist within an individual, challenges are everywhere,every marriage, everything we operate as a human being. We can only totally avoid challenges when we are died and buried

Secret 4
Every marriage has different levels of success. Don't compare your marriage with any one else. We can never be equal. Some will be far, some behind. To avoid marriage stresses, be patient, work hard and with time your marriage dreams shall come true. I have witnessed a marriage where by the wife is earning more then the husband and the husband is cool with it, but in some cases the men don't buy the idea of their wives making more money than them which is primitive if you ask me. It does not matter who's making more money everything is base on understanding,learned people don't buy the idea of wives been submissive just because of money or not making enough to stand on her own, Marriage shouldn't be base on what I can give you it's based on what we both can do together, it baffles me when I have a man saying "I want my wife to be a housewife because when she start earning money she will loss her respect for me as the head of the house very funny, a woman would loss her respect even if she depends on you for survival,it's not always about money or what u can give
Forget feminism I support the idea of a working class wife make your own money while I make mine, we can both run the affair. Again dear men whether or not your wife is working still give her money buy her gifts make her feel loved and then wait for her to reciprocate
No bad wife anywhere,she didn't change from being your sweetheart while you were dating to being a thing of regret now that you are both married lol she's not a witch waiting to ruined your life,something brought that nagging,overbearing wife you have there why not try to fix it,ask her what the problem is then allow her explain while she's explaining don't interrupt don't try to justify your actions right away just be calm and allow her moment,women likes a listener be patient enough for her to finish. When she's done with explanation you can now come in to explain yourself while explaining try not to make it confrontational and avoid shouting talk calmly.If you wanna solve a problem be diplomatic about it,make her see your reasons and then say "Sorry" not just sorry say I am sorry for doing this and that mention the problem.
My dear woman don't seat there and think you are allergic to apologizing when you are wrong,understand you can't always be right all the time. When you are wrong endeavor to say am sorry for saying this or doing that,Men are human you know don't treat them like they were created to please you,they also want to be pampered too
Don't ever be a problem to your husband because you claim to be a feminist,feminism isn't to disrespect your spouse being equal does not mean you should neglect a man as the head of the family. Men loves respect they love to feel in charge, they love superiority just give him nothing hurts a man more than being unable to control his spouse or being disrespected

Secret 5

To get married is declaring war. When you get married you must declare war against enemies of marriage. Some enemies of marriage are

IGNORANCE: Ignorance [n.]: The condition of being ignorant; the want of knowledge in general, or in relation to a particular subject; the state of being uneducated or uninformed. Ignorance in marriage has caused so many divorce and separation in marriages,there is no relationship or marriage with some level of understanding that is why courtship is very important before marriage so the both partners will understand each other well enough because what u don't know can kill you remember when they said "ignorance is a disease" this isn't a lie ignorance will kill you before your illness does,like they say knowledge is power" what you know will guide you but in a situation where you know nothing about what you are doing that can be devastating and disastrous

Whatever you are getting yourself into try as much as possible to acquire knowledge,be enlightened about it before venturing into it,marriage,work,skills and even relationships.rushing in and out would be a total waste of time so it's advisable to read,learn,ask questions from people who knows or have more experience before you go into it.

UNFORGIVING:before you even think of getting married please ask God for the spirit of forgiveness because this is the most important aspect of dealing with human if you can't forgive you can't heal you can't move pass anything at all.You will be depressed, annoyed and frustrated if you can forgive people, you can't even be genuinely happy because a lot is bottled up in your mind

Unforgiving spirit can destroy your marriage your relationship even the way you associate with people. The Bible even taught us how important it is to be able to forgive according to the Bible you have to forgive at least 77 times and even more,if you can't forgive the people you see how do u expect God to forgive you. OUR LORDS PRAYER says FORGIVE US OUR TRESPASSES AS WE FORGIVE THOSE WHO TRESPASS AGAINST US. How will you expect God in heaven to forgive you when you can't even forgive another person

Someday ago my boyfriend cheated on me while I was on holiday in another city and I found out about it,I couldn't bare the humiliation so I confronted him initially he denied it after so many quarrel he was forced to acknowledge it and he begged for forgiveness but it still wasn't enough for me. I couldn't just forgive him because I had an unforgiving spirit.each time you had an argument I will always bring it up at the end we both got fed up and broke up. You see this is something a little forgiveness could fix but know it didn't because I failed to give it a chance.We can prevent a lot from going sour if we can forgive,forgiving does not make you weak or stupid it makes you a peacemaker,it gives you happiness and prevents depression

CHEATING: A major problem in marriages now

adulterous; cheating; two-timing: not faithful to a spouse or lover (ex: adulterous husbands and wives; a two-timing boyfriend

Cheating is between both husband,wife,girlfriend or boyfriend generally people in a union,cheating isn't only having an affair with an external body cheating can be in different form you don't necessarily have to be involved sexually with anyone else to call it cheating. Cheating can be flirting,talking dirty with someone you are not sexually involved with,fantasizing about someone else for be cheating, having affair online is also cheating,having female best friends can equally reason to cheating in a relationship

Studies have found that men are more likely to engage in extramarital sex if they are unsatisfied sexually, while women are more likely to engage in extramarital sex if they are unsatisfied emotionally.
Differences in sexual infidelity as a function of gender have been commonly reported. It is more common for men compared to women to engage in extradyadic relationships. The National Health and Social Life Survey found that 4% of married men, 16% of cohabiting men, and 37% of dating men engaged in acts of sexual infidelity in the previous year compared to 1% of married women, 8% of cohabiting women, and 17% of women in dating relationships.These differences have been generally thought due to evolutionary pressures that motivate men towards sexual opportunity and women towards commitment to one partner (for reasons such as reproductive success, stability, and social expectations). In addition, recent research finds that differences in gender may possibly be explained by other mechanisms including power and sensations seeking. For example, one study found that some women in more financially independent and higher positions of power, were also more likely to be more unfaithful to their partners.In another study, when the tendency to sensation seek (i.e., engage in risky behaviours) was controlled for, there were no gender differences in the likelihood to being unfaithful. These findings suggest there may be various factors that might influence the likelihood of some individuals to engage in extradyadic relationships, and that such factors may account for observed gender differences beyond actual gender and evolutionary pressures associated with each.

STINGINESS: a lack of generosity; a general unwillingness to part with money.
love is sharing, how do you prove you love someone without giving?? My love language is gift if you can give me giftes I assume you don't love me that much
You can't be stingy to people you claim to love,if you find it difficult to give to your loved ones then you are considered stingy
Nowadays stinginess can be a hindrance in your relationship and marriage even the Bible said "GIVE AND IT SHALL BE GIVEN UNTO YOU"

It's a promise from God givers never lacks.Giving is very important in your relationship,don't be stingy to your partner except if you don't have as long as you have it give out and never expect anything in return
Generally speaking if you are in a position where you are made pay bills by your spouse because you are working please help out don't say because you are a lady your husband should be the one paying the bills nothing is wrong with helping out .we don't also forget to get your husbands gifts especially if they've been getting you gifts don't be too uptight about giving

DISRESPECT:showing lack of respect ,having no respect for someone or something
Signs of disrespect can sometimes be evident on the first date but many times don't occur until later on in the relationship. We will look at seven signs of disrespect using fictional characters and scenarios.

1.) The first sign is often a lack of regard for the other's freedom and space. After a year of dating in college, Emmy would get angry with Tom when he would spend time with his guy friends or if he was too busy to spend time with her because of school work.

2.) Another sign is a lack of respect for the other's time. Antonio consistently made his wife, Maya, late for important events, like weddings or graduation ceremonies, where it was very important to be on time. Even though Maya discussed with Antonio her desire and need to be on time, he continuously displayed a lack of regard for his wife's need.

3.) A third sign is a lack of attentiveness to the other's need for safety. Bill took Victoria for a ride on his new motorcycle on their second date. He started popping wheelies while driving at a dangerously fast speed around corners which made Victoria very uncomfortable. She continuously pleaded for Bill to stop and slow down, but he kept on.

4.) Fourth is a lack of consideration of boundaries. After three years into the relationship with Dustin, Beth looked through his phone and bedside table drawer almost on a daily basis. When Dustin looked like he was in deep thought, Beth insisted he tell her what he was thinking. Beth did not respect Dustin's right to privacy, to have his own things, even the right to not always have to share his thoughts.

5.) A need to always be right is another sign of disrespect. Harold had a large ego due to deep-seated insecurities and low self-esteem. When Harold and Martha were dating, he would not allow her to win an argument. Even if he was wrong, he would never admit he was wrong and apologize.

6.) Disrespect can also be exhibited through defensiveness. Cliff and Amy had developed a close and intimate relationship while dating, but when Cliff would attempt to give Amy constructive criticism, she would always look at it as an insult and get defensive and angry.

7.) Lastly is disrespecting need for financial security. Gerald and Lauren worked paycheck to paycheck and had established a strict budget to make sure that they were financially secure. Gerald had a shopping problem and would always buy superfluous items at the wholesale grocery. He also gambled their money playing cards with his friends, and this made Lauren very nervous.

LACK OF LOVE: relationship/marriage without love is hell unpleasant undesirable and traumatizing.A loveless marriage is a relationship where one or both partners do not feel in love.

Instead of being romantic lovers, they often feel more like roommates or siblings. Being in a loveless marriage often breeds isolation, resentment, and hopelessness.You're stuck in a loveless marriage. You and your spouse live more like roommates or platonic friends than you do husband and wife. You long for the days when you two were so madly in love you couldn't think about anything but them. Although it may be challenging to recapture that degree of infatuation, you can certainly rediscover the emotional closeness and companionship in your relationship. If you aren't willing to even consider the idea of divorce, you need to change your marriage beginning today.

The first thing you should be doing if you're stuck in a loveless marriage is talk to your spouse. Chances are very good that the two of you rarely communicate in depth. Sure you may talk about everyday things like who is going to drive the kids where or when the credit card payment is due. You need to sit down and really talk about your relationship. You should have some ground rules going into a discussion like this. Consider whether it would be a good idea to agree on the idea of not interrupting one another or deciding that you'll both try and listen and absorb rather than reacting in anger.

One of the main reasons why couples start to drift apart is they don't see each other as a priority anymore. It's understandable how this happens. With all the pressures in life it's easy to forget about what your partner needs from you. This ends up leaving behind it a trail of resentment and anger. You have to shift that if you hope to improve the marriage. Start focusing more of your time on your partner. Actually make time for them each day. That might mean working less hours or getting up earlier to share breakfast with them. You have to put in the effort to spend more time together if you want to rediscover the love that's been lost between you two

Above all else try and focus more on the positives of your partner. It's easy to fall into the trap of only looking at what you don't like about them. Doing that won't help you to feel closer to them though it will only create more emotional distance. When you feel yourself concentrating on the things about your spouse that you find unappealing you need to change your train of thought. If you have to, make a list of what you love most about them. Doing this will dramatically change the dynamic between you two and will allow you to see them in a whole new and favorable light. When you are in a long-term relationship like marriage, things will not stay the same through the years. Life becomes a routine. The demands and responsibilities of married life can take away the romance, passion and intimacy in the relationship. Lack of intimacy in a marriage can lead to different marital problems so it is important to know how to restore the intimacy in your marriage.

If there is an intimacy problem in your marriage, there are things that you can do to bring back the love and passion in your marriage.

Make yourself look good. To restore the intimacy in your marriage, you have to make time for yourself. Good grooming is important. It is easier to be intimate with your spouse if you look good and feel good about yourself. Take care of your appearance and you will get surprised on how it can have a positive effect on your relationship with your spouse.

Regular talk with your spouse. It is important to talk to each other all the time to restore the intimacy in your marriage. Talking with each other regularly will prevent misunderstandings and other conflicts. Sharing thoughts, experiences and interests will make the relationship stronger. Couples who regularly talk to each other are creating a stronger and intimate relationship.

Always create new memories. Doing the same things everyday can make the marriage dull and lifeless. To restore intimacy in your marriage, you both have to create new memories. Discover new things with your spouse to restore the intimacy in your marriage. Share common hobbies or create new hobbies together to create new memories.

Start dating again. Most couples stopped dating after they got married. This should not be the case, dating and romance should continue even if you are already married. When was the last time you gave flowers to your spouse or watch movies together? Be creative and surprise your spouse with romantic ideas that will melt his or her heart.

Although it is hard to keep a marriage, it is not impossible to create a long-lasting relationship. Is your marriage in trouble?

Are you tired of living in a relationship in which you feel neglected? Many married people find themselves feeling alone and rejected by their spouse.

Secret 6

There is no perfect marriage. There is no ready made marriage. Marriage is hard work. Volunteer yourself to work daily on it. Marriage is like a car that needs proper maintenance and proper service. If this is not done it will break down somewhere exposing the owner to danger or some unhealthy circumstances. Let us not be careless about our marriages.

The sincerity of a HUSBAND is known during the sickness of his wife.

That of a WIFE is known during the financial difficulty of the husband.

True love of CHILDREN is known during the old age of the parents.

The true nature of SIBLINGS is known during distribution of inheritance.

The SINCERITY of friends is known during hard times.

True RELATIVES are known when one is far from his country, lonely or sick.

TRUE LOVE is known when there is no means of benefit.

A TRUE BELIEVER is known during times of hardship.

In all, life is the TEACHER ITSELF.

May we grow in wisdom, understanding and

Be careful so you don't hate a lovely person, because of a dirty rumour you heard about them which was created out of jealousy and envy .

Try to appreciate those who gossip about you. It's not easy for someone to leave their problems and carry yours on their head.

Forgive betrayals but be careful with them,because next time they may not spare your life .

Even if you kill yourself for some people, they will still complain that you didn't die in a proper way.

Do your best and leave the rest, you can't satisfy human beings .

If you are always worried*I about what others are saying about you, you will never be happy.

When your blessings are getting closer, your attacks become greater.

Don't look at the storm, God is the controller of all things he created, and is by your side, you're a victorious

Everybody can not love you, don't lose your peace over those who hate you.

Those who convinced people to hate you can not convince God to hate you.

Stay connected to God always.

Have confidence in God for with God all things are possible.

Secret 7

God cannot give you a complete person you desire. He gives you the person in the form of raw materials in order for you to mould the person that you desire. This can only be achieved through prayer, love and Patience

You have to work it out yourself,make your marriage work because God didn't create a perfect being God created an imperfect being so we can create or mould ourselves to our taste.Don't stay there waiting for a perfect husband or wife because there is none anywhere.we just have to put in work,prayers and determination to ripe the perfect union you desire

Secret 8

Getting married is taking a huge risk. You can not predict what will happen in the future. Situations may change so leave room for adjustments. Husband can lose his good job or you may fail to have babies.

All these require you to be prayerful otherwise you might divorce.

People marry young, share good and bad times, have a family, begin to fight, and have sex less often as they age. Suddenly they feel alone when they are with their partner. What happened? Generally, if you recognize a problem in your relationship and are willing to take steps to change your bad habits, you can fix the marriage. However, it takes two to make a marriage work so if one spouse has his or her foot out the door, it can be difficult to fix a marriage.

1. Communication Issues

The most common complaint among married couples is lack of communication. Many couples put up with problems rather than try to fix them. In the beginning they agreed he would earn money and she would take care of the house and kids. When they face new challenges later on, they have to negotiate a new compact. The issue is whether spouses can listen to each other's complaints without interrupting or getting defensive and reach anew consensus. COMMUNICATION !!!

Effective communication is one of the major life lessons we all need to learn.

It's vital for a great marriage, and goes hand in hand with a healthy one. It's the key to a successful marriage.

Effective communication means you both understand each other when you communicate.

The earlier you learn how to communicate with your spouse, the better off your marriage will be.

WHY?

Because communication problems are the main reasons, or root cause, of the top issues that could cause married couples to divorce, separate, or breed unhealthy relationships.

Communicating with your spouse is not talking about the good stuff only, or when things are good. It also involves talking about the bad things and when everything seems to be falling apart.

Coming together to develop a plan of action will help you to communicate through both.

How can you fix your marriage problems if you do not communicate with each other?

You will have unresolved conflicts, be unfulfilled in your marriage, and always be thinking "is this what marriage is supposed to be?"

These marriage problems will build up over time and explode someday.

When this happens, it will not be pretty. You certainly want to avoid it! You want to be able to communicate with your spouse so you can both have a fulfilling marriage, the marriage you both dreamed about before saying, 'I Do.'

Poor communication can lead to growing apart as a couple. It also impacts your kids since they will be learning from you.

So, teach them how to do it in a healthy way by communicating well with your spouse. This is a simple thing but requires your action and effort to make it happen.

When you are able to communicate effectively with your spouse, you will feel secure. You will not be afraid to ask questions or seek answers. And you will have a higher level of fulfillment in your marriage.

Have you ever witnessed a married couple who have had obvious communication issues? It isn't pretty.

What you may not realize is that a lot of seemingly unrelated issues stem from the lack of effective communication.

Money issues, fights over being too busy, not busy enough, who does what around the house, starting a family, how many children to have, sex, connecting together, parenting, intimacy.

Communication is integral to everything you do with your spouse and in your marriage.

In order to improve communication in your marriage the desire and willingness of you and your spouse is needed. It will take intentional effort from you and your spouse to communicate better in your marriage.

By learning how to effectively communicate with your spouse, you will be able to succeed in your marriage, do things you never thought possible, and excel in all different areas of your life.

Marriage is one of the greatest growing opportunities we have on this earth.

It has its ups and it has its downs, but the important thing is to learn how to grow closer together through it all as a unit.

2. Ignoring Boundaries

It's not uncommon for one spouse to try to change his or her partner. Whether it's how he or she dresses or about fundamental beliefs, trying to change your spouse will feel like a personal invasion and may trigger defensiveness oranger. Overstepping boundaries can destroy mutual trust. The result is likely to be retaliation or withdrawal from the relationship.

3.lack of sexually Intimacy

There are lots of reasons couples lose interest in sex–ranging from medical problems to emotional issues. Generally, sexual problems trigger a vicious cycle where it's difficult to want sex when you feel emotionally distant from your partner and it's difficult to feel emotionally attached without experiencing sexual intimacy. To get past sexual indifference, couples need to discuss and resolve their emotional issues.

4. Emotional or Sexual Infidelity

A common problem in many marriages is for the couple to become emotionally distant. When this happens, it's likely he or she may start looking around. Emotional infidelity can lead to adultery and cheating is destructive of a marriage. It's important for every couples to discuss and agree on what constitutes infidelity.

5. Fighting About Money

Disagreements about money are inevitable in a marriage. One spouse may want to save while the other wants to spend. Disagreement about money usually reflect different core values. To avoid these problems, it's important to discuss and agree how to handle finances.

6. Selfishness

If one spouse constantly places his or her needs above the goals and interests of the marriage, it's only a matter of time before the neglected spouse begins to feel rejected and unloved. Getting married involves give and take rather than getting your own needs met all the time. If one spouse dictates the terms of the marriage and won't compromise, that's a recipe for disaster.

7. Value Differences

When a couple has core value differences, such as religious preferences, that can cause serious problems. They may have major disagreements about what religion to teach their children. Other differences include how to discipline, definitions of right and wrong, or other ethical conflicts. Everyone doesn't grow up with the same values, morals, or goals and there is lots of room for debate about right and wrong. If a couple can't learn to adjust to different values, they may have serious problems in their marriage.

8. Different Life Stages

Most couples don't think about differences in life stages when they marry, but this can be a significant problem with couples are different ages. Personalities change and a couple may not remain compatible as they transition to different life stages. An older husband may not be interested in beginning a new family while the young bride is anxious to have a baby, or he may be nearing retirement and want to slow down while she needs to stay active.

9. Boredom

Doing the same old thing can get tiresome and it's hard to make changes in a comfortable relationship until it's too late. Doing something new from time to time can add spark and spice to a relationship.

10. Jealousy

Being jealous can turn a marriage sour, especially if the jealous feelings are unrealistic. Jealous persons can become overbearing and controlling or angry and rejecting. If you are feeling jealous, see a counselor to decide wither your feelings are reasonable. You may have an attachment problem that needs to be discussed with a competent counselor.

Secret 9

Marriage is not a contract. It is permanent. It needs total commitment. Love is the glue that sticks the couple together. Divorce start in the mind and the devil feeds the mind. Never ever entertain thoughts of getting a divorce. Never threaten your spouse with divorce. Choose to remain married. God hates divorce.MARRY SOMEONE WHO IS PROUD OF YOU! Don't let anyone make you feel like you are worthless

If you don't have anything they can be proud of, you are not a husband/wife material!

Marriage was created to HELP you fulfil your vision.

Pursuing your vision with passion is what makes them pursue you with passion because passionate people command extraordinary results!

Nay! You don't need to be on the international scene before commanding results -one life touched here, business pursued with vigour there, career exploits here, spiritual acumen there, educational excellence here, talents highly developed there and on and on and on!

If all you do is chat senselessly on WhatsApp or Facebook from morning till night,Walk to and fro your street like the devil looking for who to tempt or you lay down and watch porn like someone they swear for! You need deliverance not marriage! You are not a person worth marrying, talkless of being proud of!

Proud of you, for what?

Develop your capacity for greatness! Invest in your dreams! Embark on the journey of a glorious destiny! Start doing something worthwhile with your life then you will start commanding the attention of great men/women who want to be part of your dreams and help you achieve greatness!

Secret 10

Every marriage has a price to pay. Marriage is like a bank account. It is the money that you deposit that you withdraw. If you don't deposit love, peace and care into your marriage, you are not a candidate for a blissful home.

WHAT KIND OF A WOMAN ARE YOU TO YOUR MAN?

1. THE COMPLAINING TYPE
Are you constantly whining and discontent? Do you make it so hard for your man to please you? Lady relax, you will never be happy in life if you pay more attention to what you lack than what you have

2. THE JEALOUS TYPE
Are you insecure, unsettled when your man works or even talks with female friends? Lady relax, your man is a good man that's why you chose him. He is your man. No other woman will take your place. Be secure as his queen

3. THE MOTHER TYPE
Are you treating your man like he is a boy? Telling him what to do, how to do it, and when to do it? Do you correct him as if you are disciplining a child? Do you touch him like a man or handle him like a boy? Lady, men love to be treated like grown men. Be a mother to your child but treat your man like a capable king

4. THE NEEDY TYPE
Are you too dependent and clingy? Do you choke your man with you demands, demanding your man to talk to you every 10 minutes despite you knowing he is genuinely busy? Do you suffocate your man in need of abnormal attention? Lady relax, don't push him to the edge

5. THE PUSHY TYPE
Are you living in tomorrow? Forcing your man to go to the next step when today is fresh. Are you the type to meet a new man and you are already pushing for love, then as soon as you start dating you push him to propose, then you quickly want marriage? Lady relax, you will miss out on the proper growth of love because of your haste. Love is a process not a race

6. THE TOUCHY TYPE
Are you the type who loves to touch, to hold hands, to have your hand on your man? If your man doesn't understand you he might find your touchiness too much. Hopefully the man you choose loves to be touched alot

7. THE VICTIM TYPE
Are you the lady who loves attention by dwelling on your problems, so that your man feels sorry for you? Do you find comfort in presenting yourself as the victim and how unfair the world is to you? Lady, this self-pity to gain attention is not healthy. You can't do this for long without your man feeling drained. Work on yourself

8. THE BOSSY TYPE
Do you give orders and commands, you never listen to your man, it always has to be your way? Lady, tame yourself; your man reads this as you being disrespectful

9. THE CHILDISH TYPE

It's wonderful to be fun and silly at times. But lady, look at your man's reaction to tell whether there are things you do that he finds too childish

10. THE SUICIDE TYPE
Are you manipulative, daring that you will do something life threatening so that you armtwist your man? This is the quickest way to make your man want as little as possible to do with you. You have inner problems, deal with them

11. THE IRRATIONAL TYPE
Do you rush into making regrettable decisions. Is your tongue lose to speak words that you haven't thought through? Do you do things that you will not be proud of? Do you keep changing your mind making you look unstable? Lady, a man who loves you will love you despite this weakness. But work on being an emotionally stable woman who is patient and thinks things through. This will help you in love and in life

12. THE OVER-THINKING TYPE
Do you worry too much? Are you not at peace because of over-thinking? When your husband is making love to you, do your many thoughts keep you from enjoying your husband? When enjoying quality time with your man, does your mind wander going all over the place? Lady relax, over-thinking robs you the beauty of precious real-time moments

13. THE SUSPICIOUS TYPE
Are you treating your man like a criminal, quick to assume your man is cheating or doing wrong? Do you snoop on him, put him on the spot for no reason? Does your tone suggest you don't trust him. It hurts a man when his woman doesn't believe him

14. THE LOST TYPE
Do you lose yourself in the relationship/marriage, you have no drive, no vision? Are you escorting your man in life and have nothing to live for on your own? Lady, find you. Your man doesn't want an escort or a rubber stamp, he wants an equal partner

15. THE PERFECT LOVER BUT PATHETIC FRIEND TYPE
You are good at doing things lovers do. You say romantic things, go out on dates, kiss; but you two are not true friends. You are not free with him, you would rather share your challenges and issues with another person. Lady, be not only lovers, be the best of friends

16. THE WAR-MONGERER TYPE
Are you combative, constantly looking for a fight? Lady relax, simmer down. Your man wants to be loved, not attacked

17. THE SECRETIVE TYPE
Do you keep things from your man because you think your man can't handle it or because you fear your man won't love you if he knows? Trust your man, open up

18. THE EXTREME FEMINIST TYPE
Feminism is a good thing, but have you abused it? Have you concluded in your heart that men are the enemy, that this a gender war? This negative attitude will cause you to want to prove ponts and drive your man away. Lady relax, allow yourself to receive some masculine love as you give your feminine love

19. THE I AM ALWAYS RIGHT TYPE
Do you always have to win? Do you stop at nothing to show how your way is best? Lady relax, love is about talking things out, listening, compromising and making joint decisions

20. THE LOVING TYPE
This is the type every man needs. A woman who is dependable, caring, secure, thoughtful, mature, giving, nurturing, challenging. She brings out the best in her man. Lady, keep loving him like you always do

SACRIFICES FOR YOUR MARRIAGE

Not always being right
As a human you can't also be right even when you are don't make the other look stupid
I love to be right and hate to be wrong, but I've learned to give up being right all the time for the sake of my marriage. Conflicts in marriage aren't always black and white with one person on the right side and one person on the wrong side. Marriage forces you to learn to see conflict from someone else's point of view, and, hopefully, from there you can give up your entitlement to always being right.

Having the ultimate say-so in dinner and entertainment choices.

Chick flick or action movie? Chinese food or Italian food? When you get married, you can't always have your cake and eat it too. You learn to compromise or to take turns choosing where to eat or what to watch on TV. It's not a huge sacrifice, but sometimes it can feel like it.

Sharing the bed.

A queen-sized bed is not as big as it may seem. It gets even smaller when you're married and have animals or kids that join you in the middle of the night. It's the elbow in the face at 3 a.m. or waking up to realize you don't have any covers – that's the real sacrifice of sharing a bed. A king sized bed helps with that, but it still doesn't keep you from dealing with your spouse's snoring or his or her alarm going off and waking you up before you have to be awake.

Choosing how you spend your free time.

This isn't a huge deal before couples have kids because both people can pretty much do whatever they want, but when you add kids to the equation, it gets a little trickier. You learn to plan ahead and to trade off watching the kids, but you may still miss out on fun times with friends every now and then.

Splitting holidays with family and in-laws.

Making holidays work for both sides of the family isn't as easy as it sounds, and it can be hard to give up spending time with your family in favor of spending time with your in-laws. The best thing to do is to remember that it's just as hard for your in-laws to share their daughter or son with your family too.

Dealing with someone else's messes.

Marriage means dealing with double the dishes, double the trash, double the laundry, and double the mess. Sometimes the weight of that mess falls equally on both people, and sometimes there is one person who tidies up more than the other. When you're the tidier one, the other person's mess can feel like a burden, and it can be a sacrifice to deal with the other person's messes.

Making financial decisions as a team.

I'm a saver, and I married a spender. If I had it my way, we would save just about every penny because you never know when those rainy days might come. I've learned to compromise here and there, and so has he. Sharing money and making financial decisions together isn't always easy, but we're both better off when we are on the same page together.

The truth is marriage is full of sacrifices – more than just those listed here. Marriage takes work, and sacrificing for the other person is just part of that, and while it might not always be easy, it's certainly a small price to pay to be with the person you love the most.

HOW TO AVOID BEING MANIPULATED WHILE CHOOSING A LIFE PARTNER!!!

Dear waiting single bachelors and spinsters, manipulation is real, don't fall for it.

One thing that I have discovered recently is that when God has great plans for your life, the devil is also not sleeping. You need to be very careful, patient, and prayerful to avoid becoming its victim.

Manipulation is the process of planning out usually with subtle skill, deceit or care so that your choice of who to marry is influenced by the manipulator, to their own advantage.

A manipulator would influence you emotionally to do their bidding. They will tell you, "Marry this person," or "This is the person I want you to marry," please be careful.

The devil also manipulates through the agency of his representatives disguised as men or women of God, or some spiritual fathers or mothers, or counselors.

Be careful of making anyone an assistant to God in your life.

How can I escape being a victim of manipulation?

1) Be spiritually sensitive: Becoming spiritually alert is not by going to church or praying once in a while, it is by having a functional prayer altar, and becoming so addicted to the word of God that you study and meditate in it as commanded.

The fact remains that you are going to fall into satanic manipulation when you make marital decision during the prayerless season of your life.

If the iron be blunt, then you do well to sharpen it. If your spirit man can't clearly discern God's voice above the storms of passion, and the murmurs of self-will, it's advisable to sharpen up your inner man.

Take time to develop your prayer life, pray always and don't faint. Spend quality time with God, not just when you need Him urgently.

2) Don't let anyone influence your choice on whom to marry. Whether good decision or bad is what you ended up making, you will face the consequence. Don't let anyone influence you on who to marry.

You might be told she has money, he's working in a bank, he or she is romantic, he's nice, she's humble, and so on; until you clearly hear God, don't make any move.

Be it a man of God, prophet or seer, let no one be the final influence on who you marry, else you'd discover later in marriage that you have married the wrong person.

It's better to be very slow and get it right than to hurriedly make decisions, and regret it afterwards.

3) Don't get so involved with anyone that you would accept anything they tell you, hook, line, and comprehend without accepting it.

Similarly to point 2, don't make anyone in your life infallible, the only person that can't make error is God.

Do you know that some men or women of God are not in their best state spiritually to guide you?

A man of God is first a man before the grace of God comes upon his life.

No marriage counselor or relationship coach knows it all or understand God's will for you. The crux of this matter is to never make anyone an idol in your life that you worship or treasure their counsel above that of God and His word.

4) Never be in haste or under pressure to get married. One of the greatest strategies that make singles manipulated is when they see themselves as getting old or late to be married.

If it would cost you more than a month to propose or accept a proposal, while prayerfully seeking His face for direction, please do, and take your time.

A genuine brother won't hurry you to accept his proposal, and a sincere sister won't delay your proposal for ages.

5) Invoke the mercy of God. I have come to believe that those who marry right do not do so, because they can pray or fast very well, it's a token of God's mercy.

Let God take away His mercy, they'll miss it just as a person misses his or her last opportunity in life.

Inasmuch as you would pray, don't fail to invoke His mercy so that when every other things seems to be right or perfect, His mercy would prevail and you would see clearly.

Dear reader, manipulation is real. One major reasons why serious and firebrand brothers and sisters missed it in their choice of who to marry is because they became a victim of satanic deception and manipulation.

Deception and manipulation goes side by side, and Satan is often the instigator. He provoked David, and made him to number the children of Israel. Subtly, the old prophet deceived the young prophet while thinking it was the will of God for him to do his bidding.

Don't make any decision when you are confused or uncertain. Let no one rush you!

MARRIAGE IS SWEETEST WHEN YOU MARRY YOUR BEST FRIEND

MARRIAGE without friendship is just a MISCARRIAGE.

MARRY your FRIEND, and BEFRIEND who you MARRY, this is true, But you must understand that for such to happen, you must be a friendly person yourself.

You should know how to laugh, smile and let things go easily.

You that is always keeping face like plastic, you better repent

Oga that is looking for wife that will worship him, wife that will call him "Lord and Master Superior", is that how you want to marry your friend?

Your Partner will call you baby, and you get angry, because you are not a baby, she should call you Sir, is that how you will marry your friend?

Small joke, you have vex

Small play, you start feeling insulted and start talking about age and who is the head and who is the tail.

You that doesn't listen or take your partners advice, as if you have ear infection
Small quarrel, you'll keep malice for one full month as if it is data subscription.
Want to be friendly with your Partner?
Come down from your high horse.
Drop the age difference
Drop your ego, your status/position in society, your headship or whatever, be humble and just be FRIENDS
I love soft love, where we communicate as adults, resolve conflicts amicably, apologize when wrong, compromise healthily, understand ourselves, have same values, pray together, push ourselves to be better and spoil ourselves. Just two adults making their lives easy.

SEX IN MARRIAGE

Sex is the most important aspect in a marriage. Initially, the love and attraction is what plays a crucial role in holding the relationship together, however, with time, sex becomes significant in ensuring the longevity of a relationship. Without any sexual activity, there will be everything but intimacy.

There is difference between sex and love making

People actually get tired of sex, but no one gets tired of love making
Sex only has to do with the genitals
But love making the genitals do not matter the couple spend time exploring each other which give birth to more bonding and intimacy between a couple
In love making new things are learnt every day and a couple wishes tomorrow's own be better then today
Sex is all about Orgasm and rounds and one partner may be satisfied leaving the other hanging
In love making Orgasm and rounds doesn't count, although orgasms may come love making focuses more on total fulfillment and it makes sure both parties comes out fully satisfied and yearning for another time they may meet to explore each over and over again.

LOVE LANGUAGES

The five love languages are the different ways in which we express that we love someone.

Most languages have ways beyond words to express yourself. The same goes for love: There are different ways to show it :

1. *Words of Affirmation.*
 Words of praise and encouragement are a powerful way to share love for someone.
To speak this language, you give verbal compliments often.
Make sure they know you love their smile, their sense of humor, or that new outfit.

2. *Quality Time.*
 Work and busy lives can get in the way of this love language all too easily.
 We can be in the same room as our partner and still fail to actually 'be' with them because of our electronics.

The key to quality time is undivided attention.
It can either be quality conversations or quality activities with your partner, like date night.

3. *Gift Giving.*
For some, gifts are a physical symbol of how their partner feels about them.
Remember that it doesn't matter how much it costs; it's just the act of going out and getting or making a gift for your partner that will show them how you feel about them.

4. *Acts of Service.*
This is helping your partner with the things with which you know they would appreciate help.
It can be things like helping the kids with homework, doing bills, or vacuuming, and will be different for everyone.

5. *Physical Touch.*
Even in infancy, humans need physical touch to thrive.
We often forget, but this carries on into adulthood as well.
Some ways you can express love in this way are holding hands, cuddling, kissing, or sex. Of course, find out what kinds of physical contact they like most, and this will deepen your intimacy.

DEAR WIFE

If you don't use sex as a weapon to punish your husband and teach him a lesson; your husband will learn to build intimacy with you.

If you complain less and appreciate your husband more; he will enjoy your company and spend time with you more.

If you do not overreact about issues; your husband will confide in you more.

If you learn to tell your husband what is bothering you as opposed to keeping quiet and being moody; he will be able to solve issues with you.

If you learn to trust your husband without accusing him falsely, he will share with you about his female friends and colleagues.

If your demeanor is peaceful and not combative; your husband will look forward to coming home to you.

If you respond positively to your husband's flirts; he will enjoy being naughty with you.

If you care about his well-being and how his day has been as much as you want him to ask you "How was your day?"; he will not feel alone.

If you don't keep a record of wrongs, reminding him of what he did in the past; your husband will be motivated to invest more in a future with you.

If you don't praise another man more than your husband in his presence be it your pastor, colleague or celebrity; he will not feel insecure.

If you are confident about your body and beauty; your husband will find you extremely sexy.

If you don't tell him things like "You are not man enough", "You are a failure"; he will not feel attacked.

If you thank him for the little he has done; he will do more for you.

If you don't equate his value as a man to the money he has or doesn't have; he will be real with you and see a life partner who notices all of him in you.

HOW TO SEXUALLY TEASE YOUR WIFE/HUSBAND

Marriage is good when you have a spouse that makes your blood run. Here are ways to tease your spouse and keep him/ her thirsty for you

1. BUY GOOD BRAS

Ladies, men have a thing for boobs. It does not matter how small or big your breasts are, men have a thing for their shape and nipples. Invest in a good bra, find what works for your breasts. No one else gets to see your breasts, so wear a bra that he will look at and want to undress you

2. WORK OUT WITH YOUR SPOUSE

There is something sexy about jogging, push ups, sit ups, sweat, tight sports wear pants that teases the eyes. Work out with your spouse, he/she will see your body movements as you exercise and desire you

3. SHOW THE FULLNESS OF YOUR CROUCH

Gentlemen, wear a nice fitting boxer, the kind that shows your penis loaded inside. She will see you walking around in it in the bedroom and want to strip you. Yes, women love eye candy too

4. FLIRT ON THE PHONE

When you are both far from each other, send naughty messages to each other. Stimulate your spouse even when distance separates you. Let it be that when your spouse thinks of making love he/she thinks of you. Grown ups think of love making a lot

5. KISS PLAYFULLY

Don't rush the kisses. Play with the tongue, prolong the kisses. Make your spouse relax

6. GRAB HER BUTT
Whether she has a big or small butt; creep up from behind her as she cooks, works or moves about the house. Women love it when their husband hold and touch them confidently in a way that makes her feel wanted

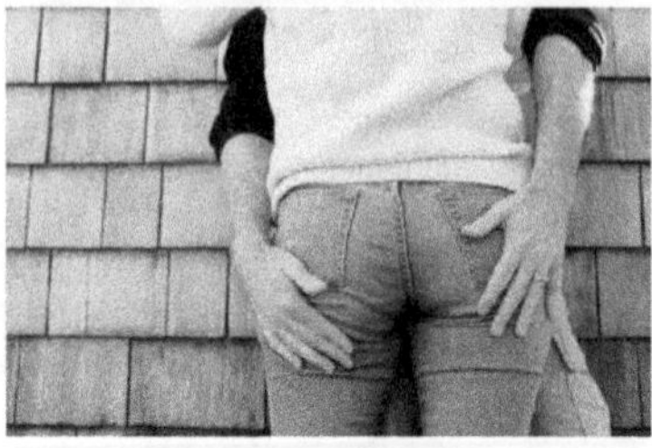

7. TOUCH THE CENTRE OF HIS PANTS
Dear wife, your husband's penis belongs to you. Out of the blue, place your hand on his pants and rub it gently. Even if he is busy, tease him so that he knows he is about to get some good loving once he is done with work or, he can get some of your good loving then get back to work

8. MAKE OUT
So many married people don't make out, they just go straight into orgasms. Create quality time for making out where you kiss as your hands move on each other's body. Rub, touch, feel. Take your time

9. WHISPER FANTASIES
Whisper into your spouse's ear the things you will do for him/her. It's a shame how so many married people text to other people their sexual fantasies yet they find it difficult to tell them to their spouse. Turn on your spouse, not other men/women

10. MASSAGE
Your fingers are one of the most powerful teasing weapons. Let your spouse lie down and massage him/her. Release all the tension in his/her body then touch the erogenous spots on his/her skin. Notice how he/she gets excited then insist that he/she should relax, you are not yet done

11. BEND OVER IN FRONT OF HIM
Ladies, you have something your husband wants behind you. Deliberately position your butt in front of him. Bend, wear tights when with him, show your curves. Show off your butt to him, he doesn't need the butt of the women walking in the streets

12. BE PLAYFUL
Adults also have games. Let him chase you as he sees your breasts jumping up and down. Lay her down and come on top of her and tell her how beautiful she looks. Blind fold him and place his hands on parts of your body and tell him to guess what part of your body he is touching. Play a game of strip poker

13. SLEEP NAKED
As you two talk, the visible and easy to reach nipples, butt, curves, penis and vagina will be a strong tease

14. MAKE NAUGHTY JOKES
Talk suggestively to your spouse

15. BREATHE ON YOUR SPOUSE
Your voice and how you breathe can be such a turn on

16. PUSH UP YOUR BODY ON HIM
When you two are sleeping, position your butt on his penis, allow him to feel your curve

May your sex life be enjoyable. But remember, all these only work when you treat your spouse well when sex is not involved. How much your spouse finds you sexy depends on how you treat him/her.

IMPORTANT EMOTIONAL NEEDS

I have identified ten basic emotional needs that are usually expected to be met in marriage: affection, sexual fulfillment, conversation, recreational companionship, honesty and openness, physical attractiveness, financial support, domestic support, family commitment, admiration.

We experience pleasure when they're met and frustration when they're not.

While almost everyone has these ten emotional needs to some extent, people vary greatly in the way they prioritize them.

For some, the need for sex is the most important of the ten, while others place the greatest priority on admiration.

Whichever need is considered most important, that's the one that deposits the most love units when it's met (and withdraws the most when it's unmet).

It isn't necessary for couples to meet all of these needs.

If a couple simply learns to meet each other's most important emotional needs, they can have a fulfilling marriage.

What are your spouse's emotional needs?

I listed ten basic needs common to most of us. But one of the most important discoveries I made, was that men and women tend to put these needs in a very different order.

Men tend to give the highest priority to:

1. Sexual fulfillment

2. Recreational companionship

3. Physical attractiveness

4. Domestic support

5. Admiration

Women, on the other hand, tend to give the highest priority to:

1. Affection

2. Conversation

3. Honesty and openness

4. Financial support

5. Family commitment

Of course, not every man or woman prioritizes the needs the same way.
Many men make affection or conversation one of their top five needs, and many women rank admiration and sexual fulfillment among their most important needs.
But on average, men and women rank these needs in the ways I've listed.
Since the emotional needs of men and women are so different, no wonder they have difficulty adjusting in marriage!

A man can set out to meet his wife's needs, but he will fail miserably if he assumes her needs are the same as his.
Women will also fail if they assume their husbands have the same needs women have.
I have seen this simple error threaten many homes.
A husband and wife fail to meet each other's needs, not because they're selfish or uncaring, but because they are ignorant of what those needs are.
You cannot assume that your spouse's needs are in the same order
of priority as yours.
If you are like most couples, your most important emotional needs are probably quite different.
But whether or not you're like most couples, you are the only one who can identify your most important emotional needs.
Only you know what your spouse can do to give you the best feelings possible.

In the same way, your spouse is the best expert on his or her needs, so as you

HOW TO CARE FOR HUSBAND

Take care of him
The reality about relationships is that it is not one person's responsibility to take care of the other. It is a mutual or collective responsibility. Partners must do their best to take care of one another. Talking to him whenever he opens up because it shows you are listening and caring Indulging in romantic gestures since men find it special Making him feel less insecure to avoid him getting glum or avoiding you.

~Enhance what made him attracted to you!
Men get attracted to women in different ways. It could be your smile, your looks of love, your body type, or your interactions. One of your girlfriend duties is to enhance the things that got him attracted to you. Figure out the various ways of letting him see more of them so that he can remember how amazing you are.

~Motivate him Knowing how to treat your boyfriend or husband well is not enough if you are not motivating him. As a girlfriend or a wife, you possess some unique powers that can inspire your man to help him to achieve his potential. Men tend to behave masculinely. But it is the selfless love of his woman that makes him want to change and become better.

~Luxuriate him in a public and private, display of affection! Men appreciate some form of light physical contact from the women they have a love interest. Although men do not care about a public display of affection, they love it when it is their girlfriend or wife that does it. Holding his hand, putting your arm around him, and touching him fondly makes him gain insights into your thoughts of him.

~Make him happy
One of the best qualities of a good girlfriend or wife is making her man/king □ happy. It is one of the top responsibilities in a relationship. You can make your man happy by:

♥□Finding out what he wants from you
♥□Not ignoring him even when he is with his friends
♥□Praising him all times even in front of others ♥□Satisfying him emotionally and sexually□

~Be there as a support system

It is natural for men to act strong. That is despite many of them suffering and tearing apart from inside. If you want to know how to become a good girlfriend or wife, make it your responsibility to support him whenever he is undergoing or facing a difficult time. Do not expect him to tell you what he is going through because men do not like looking weak. But encourage him to open up and show him support. He will come around and open up

~Be a good listener
In any girlfriend-boyfriend relationship or marriage, one of the best qualities a lady can have is to listen to their partner and comprehend whatever they are telling each other. As a good girlfriend or wife, understand that you may not be in a position to solve all of your man's problems. Since he realises this, be there to listen to him. It will make him feel that he is not alone.

Support and help him achieve his goals, by bringing out the best in him

Words are like a flying bullet, it can never return back when triggered, either to kill or to spare so be careful how you use it even though it is free.

There are words you don't need to use on your wife /husband no matter what. Control your anger, remember what happened to brother Moses upon all his good work he miss the promise land.

There are words you will use to your wife/husband and it will remain in his/her mind and against you forever so be careful.

Calling your wife a prostitute, even though you find him in such act, handle your temper, it is here that your love and qualities will be reviewed. Abusing him/her, you have pushed me to the wall, after reaction what will be your gain?

Anything you do in anger you must regret it, please be careful.

Again, nothing kills a man/woman than sharing his/her property with another, question. If you love him/her why opening your legs to a strange man/woman?

Any day you Share your properties with strange one, Satan has taken over your marriage that day, confess to each other before it must be reviewed, try to understand when confessed and pray together. Don't use it against each other and move ahead.
Do that thing that is hard for other men to do to their wives/husband, wake up to receive each other while coming back, a cup of water to drink, help to dress or undress, eat together, be each others companion, chat him/her on phone even though you are present with him/her, present surprises . These are foolish things but what much in marriage.
When one is angry, never you try to be angry but control him/her, calm him/her down, when one is accusing each other, don't raise voice try to let him/her to understand or short up at that moment, latter explain.
Be careful how you talk, don't disclose your husband/wife weakness others

HOW TO CALM YOUR HUSBAND'S MIND

1. MAKE LOVE TO HIM

Sex has a way of relaxing a man. You will change his mood when you make love to him, especially if you are the one who seduces him and initiates it

2. DON'T MAKE THE HOME A WARZONE
If coming home to you is coming home to yet another argument and fight where you explode and turn everything into an issue, he will dread coming home and it hurts when home is a place to run away from, not to run to

3. ASK HIM HOW HE IS
Most women want the husband to ask them "How was your day?", "How did you sleep?" "How are you?" yet they rarely ask the husband these. If these questions make you feel cared for, your husband also wants to feel cared for

4. ORGANIZE HIS LIFE
A lot of men can be disorganized, especially when they are going through a lot in life or have a lot on their mind. This chaos in their system, dressing, schedule or environment can lead to more unease on their mind. When you help him clear the clutter and attend to some of his needs without him asking, he will think better

5. DON'T ATTACK HIS MAN CAVE
Most have a man cave. This is an activity they do or a place they go to perhaps a room; maybe to play a game, watch TV, meditate and think, write, read, create, work out or just be. Don't attack this, just agree with him on how he can balance his time so that he doesn't spend too many hours in his man cave

6. PRAY FOR HIM
You are the one who knows best his potential, struggles, battles and questions; commit him to prayer. Let him hear you pray for him

7. HELP HIM OUT FINANCIALLY
A lot of men are going through stress due to finances. Help him, by not putting pressure on him to give the family a lifestyle he can't afford at present, by helping to pay some of the bills, by helping him manage finances better, by saving and seeking long term investments, by stepping up especially when he has been fired or going through business losses

8. AFFIRM HIM
A man can get tired, a man can go through burn out, a man can question himself, a man can worry, a man can get discouraged; which is why it is important for you to remind him of his greatness, celebrate his achievements and tell him how proud you are of him. This motivates him

9. STAY FAITHFUL TO HIM
Nothing destabilizes a man like when he suspects or finds out that the wife he loves and has given his all to is entertaining, flirting, sleeping with or longing to be with another man. Spare him this torture

10. BE EASY TO TALK TO
Most men show a tough face and don't open up to anyone because they trust no one. This is how many of them go through depression and suffer in silence. They long to find a confidant who they can reveal themselves and their deepest joys and pain to; be that confidant

11. SMILE
The smile of the woman a man loves keeps him going. Your smile inspires him and makes him want to do more for you to keep it

12. KISS HIM
Kissing him shows affection. Kiss him not just on his lips, kiss his cheeks, his arms, his back as you tell him you love him

13. MASSAGE HIM
Home massages are the best. Invest in some good massage oils and ask him occasionally to lie down and give him a feel good massage. Lie down too so that he can return the favour

14. MAKE NEW MEMORIES WITH HIM
When he is spending time with you - face to face or online, make new memories together; joke with him, tease him, play with him, have stimulating conversations with him, do something new. This will recharge him and make him miss you when you two are apart

And after she does all these My Guys, PLEASE, Give her Love, Give her PLENTY PLENTY Money as your hand reach, take her on Beautiful Vacations, be Romantic, Respectful, Attentive and Considerate to her.

HOW TO BE A GOOD HUSBAND TO YOUR WIFE

This should serve as a wakeup call to all the men out there whether married or unmarried. You can always learn and prepare yourself for a better marriage before time. That time when women were married and treated like a piece of trash should have gone by now. We are now in a new era where things have taken a drastic turn. If you still get married because you need someone to cook for you, wash for you, clean your house, give birth and take care of your children, some form of sex machine where you go to them when you need them, or simply because all the people in your category have settled down, then you should surely be the only one in that class. Real men now marry for better reasons than the above mentioned. Get married because you need a companion for life, a better half and someone you can always turn to in times of happiness and when you are down. Get married because you are fully prepared and understands what it means to be married. A man and a woman are different in several ways, you need to understand this so that you will know how to treat and respond to your spouse.

But what does it really mean to be a GOOD HUSBAND? TRUST and LOYALTY are the two signs that indicate that you have a good husband. Yet there are still a number of things that a good husband needs to measure up to, to prove to you that he truly cares.

1. A husband who sets the example in the home, initiates prayers and devotions, Bible studies and takes the lead and do it first for the wife to follow is a good husband (1 Corinthians 11:3).

2. A good husband understands his wife and knows when she's happy or sad and then communicate properly to bring her out of that sad mode.

3. A husband who consults his wife during decision making and trust his wife's own point(s) of view is a good husband.

4. A husband who acknowledges that house chores is not an easy task and helps the wife from time to time in cleaning, cooking and taking care of the children without the wife necessarily asking for his help.

5. A good husband finds interest in the affairs of his wife, supports and encourages her to become better and build a hedge of protection round her and make her feel secure.

6. A good husband is one who stands up and supports his family, providing for them regardless of whether the wife earns a salary or not (1 Timothy 5:8).

7. A good husband is one who has the best interest of his family at heart and can't afford to be lazy and do nothing when he knows that the future of a generation is at risk.

8. A good husband creates a conducive environment at home where everyone is happy and smiles are the new normal of the home.

9. A good husband respects and trusts his wife enough and gives her time of her own.

10. A good husband doesn't wait for the wife to initiate romance, he does, he doesn't wait for the wife to crack jokes first, he does, he showers his wife with surprises and gifts randomly, he remembers the wife's special dates and favorites, he seeks to satisfy and please his wife and ensures happiness and peace stay in the home where he lays his head to have rest. This is very important as there is no place like home.

It is not easy to become this kind of husband and it cannot happen overnight too. But what is important is that you know that you need to be good and make that amazing woman by you feel thankful for choosing you. First thing is for you to know what to do and then you can always figure a way on how to do it. If you have not been a good husband for all this while that you have been married, kindly start changing the narratives. The Bible says "you should enjoy your wife in the days that you have in this meaningless life…" (Ecclesiastic 9:9a)
How often do you appreciate the good king or queen in your spouse? Do you do it sometimes, most times or you cannot remember the last day you did so? Do you know that the husband/wife you have now is the prayer point of another single man or woman out there? It is important to prove to your man/woman how important they are in your life. Remind them of the crucial part they play in your life.

Husbands need some words of affirmations too as much as wives do. When you appreciate and congratulate your husband, you boost his self-esteem and they do superseding subsequently. Likewise when you appreciate your wife for all the hard work that she puts in place to see that the home is tidy as always, she feels like doing more.

Let your spouse know you see and acknowledge the extra steps they take each day to make the marriage work and to make you happy, say a word of thank you when they offer a gift or just a mere glass of water or plate of food, look them in the eye and tell them how special they are to you, hold them tight and whisper to a word of kindness in their ears. I encourage you do this, you can start today if you haven't been doing so.

Romans 13:8: Owe no one anything, except to love each other, for the one who loves another has fulfilled the law.
Some men don't know how to say SORRY yet they love you with their all.

There are men whom because of their ego (which all men do have), won't be able to go low and apologize to you with a word of sorry. Rather, they will prefer to show you how sorry they are by performing some cheerful deeds. Many people have different feelings as far as apologizing and saying sorry is concerned. To some people, they feel compelled since perhaps they were forced from childhood to always apologize to their siblings, to others, they feel ashamed and less of themselves and yet to others, they feel so okay to freely apologize and let things.

Being in a relationship offers so many opportunities to do wrongs and so the need to apologize keeps coming up. If you want a good, strong and healthy marriage, then you "MUST" learn ways of repairing things when they seem to go wrong. It is good to learn how to properly apologize and take responsibility of your actions and the part you played in hurting your partner. But, some husbands still bypass this proper way of apologizing and adopt their own ways of going about it.

1. Some husbands will rather do all the house chores even before their wives wakeup from bed just to show how sorry they are after a clash.

2. Other husbands will present gifts and items their wives had admire some time back as a sign to make up and show they are sorry.

3. Some husbands will take their wives out and give them a special treat just to communicate in a different language that they are sorry.

4. Some husbands will dedicate a day or two off and be at home and offer their wives their undivided attention just to make up.

5. Other husbands will make breakfast in bed, cook, take care of the kids and even give the wife a massage all to show how sorry they are.

6. Some husbands will take their wives out for a picnic, to watch a movie or to a beauty salon for their wives to be made up.

In as much as proper apology is needed for a healthy marriage, whatever way your husband tries to show you how sorry he is, do not underestimate and devalue it. It takes some of them huge courage to make these moves to please you and show you they are sorry. That is why it is essential to know and understand your partner; their abilities and capabilities. Take note: only good husbands who fear God will go as far as pleasing you in the above mentioned points (Ephesians 5:25). Some won't even care if you got angry or not but remember there is nothing too hard for the Lord to do. God is capable of changing such husbands to their best versions, just trust Him (Genesis 18:14, Jeremiah 32:27).

SIGNS OF AN ARROGANT HUSBAND

We all become selfish at some points in our lives and manifest it in different situations and actions. Thus, selfishness is not something that is impossible. But when it comes to a relationship and one partner is only at the receiving end and never gives back, life can become so miserable, suffocating and frustrating to the other partner. Has your marriage gone from "we" to "I"? From caring to lack of concern? Does your husband considers only his own opinion and never cares about yours and how you feel? Then you might be having a selfish and arrogant husband. Let's take a look at the following signs of an arrogant and selfish husband:

1. An arrogant husband always looks for ways to avoid communication. Whereas for a relationship to thrive, there is a need for proper communications to resolve issues and plan for the future.

2. An arrogant husband doesn't care about your aspirations, interest, dreams and feelings. To him, they don't count and all what matters is his own actions.

3. During sex, an arrogant husband cares to please and satisfy only himself. Sexual intimacy is a very important aspect of every marriage life, it is not meant for selfish people who only care about their needs rather it is a give and take pleasure.

4. An arrogant and selfish husband will never consult you nor consider your take when making his decisions.

5. A selfish and arrogant husband doesn't even acknowledge your presence be it in private or in public. He lives his life as though he is alone and free.

6. A husband who doesn't even know if the relationship is growing healthy or unhealthy, is selfish and arrogant.

7. A husband who will prefer to cite with and support outsiders instead of his own spouse is selfish and arrogant.

8. He will never border to take you out for a romantic date or even remember your special days like your birthday, anniversary and more. Such a husband is selfish and arrogant.

9. A husband who leaves the house and never thinks of returning on time, a husband who will never give his wife a call to find out how she and the kids are doing back at home and a husband who doesn't sit to discuss with his wife on casual and serious things is a selfish and arrogant (1 Timothy 5:8).

10. An arrogant husband doesn't feel the need to apologize to his wife even if he is seriously hurting her.

An arrogant spouse can make life so unbearable for you and frustrate all your attempts to build a strong and solid relationship (2 Peter 2:9 Then the Lord knows how to rescue the godly from trials, and to keep the unrighteous under punishment until the day of judgment). You can even feel like running away to get a cool head outside. Unfortunately, running away won't help matters at all. There is always a solution to everything and how to deal with all kinds of people. Consider trying the following points if you experience the above mentioned signs:

1. Identify what has changed and might be causing him to exhibit such behaviours.

2. Talk to him frankly how you feel about his attitude.

3. Do not expect him to start apologizing so soon.

4. Pray for him always and hand him to God (Luke 1:37 For nothing will be impossible with God).

5. Try to adjust and make small changes with the hope to make him happy (Titus 2:5).

6. If things get so bad, talk to a marriage therapist or counsellor about it.

7. Work on rebuilding your marriage and start all over again.

HOW TO COPE WITH AN ARROGANT HUSBAND

Your arrogant husband probably seems to have an over-sized ego that takes pleasure in putting others down. But usually this bravado is a defense mechanism developed to cover up his lack of healthy pride and genuine self-worth. Arrogance often evolves from an attempt to compensate for some painful past experiences that lowered self-confidence, suggests clinical psychologist Michelle Roya Rad in the Huffington Post article, "How to Deal With Self-Centered People." You might be able to conjure some compassion for your husband if you remind yourself his arrogance stems from his hurt and shame.

Assert Your Rights

It's going to take a toll on your marriage if your husband frequently forces his opinions on you. Arrogant people are often competitive, manipulative and disrespectful as well, warns clinical psychologist Melanie Greenberg in the article "How to Keep Your Cool with Competitive People" on the Psychology Today website. Your husband's tactics might leave you feeling disrespected and lower your self-esteem if you don't take charge of the situation and change the dynamic between you. Assert your rights in your interactions with your husband, but don't attack him or get into arguments. Don't challenge every arrogant assumption he makes, even if you're certain you're right. Make clear I-statements about what you are feeling and thinking. Establish your boundaries and let him know what you will no longer tolerate. For example, you could inform him that the next time he disrespects you in public you will leave the room, then follow through if necessary.

Counseling

Don't rule out the option of seeking professional help. If your husband's arrogance stems from deep-seated personality flaws, he's probably having difficulty in his professional life as well as with his friends and other family members. Chances are he'll need professional help to understand what he's doing and why before he's able to change. Marriage counseling can help the two of you develop healthier ways of communicating with each other. If he refuses to seek help consider going alone so you can build your own self-esteem, learn better coping strategies and how to give him an ultimatum that might change his mind.

Stress Reduction

It's frustrating to live with arrogant behavior every day. Find ways to reduce your levels of stress. Keeping a journal might be a safe outlet for you to vent your frustration without needing to confront your husband in an argument. You might also gain insight into which specific behaviors of your husband are the most distressing for you and deal with those first. Find time to relax and have fun without your husband. For example, take a relaxing bath, go for a long walk, or meet a friend for coffee. Take care of yourself by exercising regularly, eating healthy and getting a sufficient amount of sleep.

Seek to Understand

Your spouse is likely feeling a deep sense of fear, which is likely at the root of his behavior "Dealing With Negative People," the fear of disrespect, the fear of being unlovable and the fear that the world is a dangerous place. Because your spouse is unable to see his negative attitude as his problem, he will likely continue to blame external circumstances, people and events for why he views the world in such a bleak manner. Trying to change his mind will likely drain you further.

Compassion

Place yourself in your husband's shoes. Try imagining being in his mind, with consistent negative thoughts and feelings constantly arising. The negative energy that he exudes and you can't help but absorb, resides within him at all times. This may help you to develop compassion for the person that he is, which can help you respond to him in a loving, rather than in an angry way. When your husband voices a negative comment, ask him to tell you what he means. Listen intently but avoid responding, as this may increase his negativity if he feels you are trying to change him, according to Lori Radun, author of "7 Ways to Deal With the Negative People in Your Life," published on SelfGrowth.com.

Maturity

Avoid blaming your spouse for causing you to feel unhappy, as this is counter productive, according to Raghunathan. Rather, show your spouse you are in control of your own destiny by pursuing your dreams, taking risks and forming trusting relationships. Explain the reasons for your choices when he makes a distrusting or negative remark. Take responsibility for your choices and any negativity that may personally come up in your own outlook. This can help you to avoid the negative cycle of energy and work towards increasing positive energy between the two of you.

Focus on Yourself

Realize that while you are unable to control others, you have control over your own thoughts, feelings and the way you communicate with your spouse. You may find it difficult to change the way you interact with your husband at first, but it will likely become easier with time. As you change the way you communicate, he may surprise you with less negativity. Begin by not taking his negative comments and criticism personally; negative people are generally like that with everyone, states Psych Central. This will help to change your own perception regarding his negative energy.

HOW TO PROPERLY APOLOGIZE TO YOUR PARTNER

To make a mistake as a spouse does not imply that you are a bad person all together. However, if you hope for a strong, healthy and happy marriage, then, it's important to look for long lasting ways to repair your relationship each time you wrong your spouse. Whether you hurt your partner intentionally or not, proper apology opens the way for a better communication and allows you and your spouse to set boundaries, and new rules to help guide you to avoid similar situations in the future. But what are the wrong and common ways spouses often apologize when they hurt each other?

1. Just saying "I am SORRY" without adding any other word to it is a very wrong way of apologizing. This type of apology is so self-boosting and full of pride. You are simply telling your spouse that he/she should hear it and let you be. You are not remorseful for what you did at all. However, saying SORRY intentionally can help calm down a situation for a moment.

2. Saying "if I offended you, I am SORRY" simply translates that your partner is too sensitive and shouldn't have been offended by what you did but you do not regret doing it.

3. Saying "I am SORRY you feel that way" is the worst apology ever. You are simply telling your spouse that they shouldn't have felt that way. You are only responsible for your words and actions and not another person's feelings.

4. Saying "alright, I am SORRY, are you happy now?" is no apology at all. You are simply avoiding the real issue and looking for ways to move on.

5. Saying "I am SORRY I said it that way" simply implies that what you said is correct but you just said it in the wrong way. It is not a form of apology.

Proper apology goes way beyond just saying you are SORRY. It is expressed both in words and actions and your body language says whether you are truly remorseful or not. Here is how to properly apologize when you hurt your spouse:

1. Ask your partner if he/she is ready to hear your apology just yet. Do not take the step of asking for permission for granted because your spouse might just need some little time to be ready to hear your apology.

2. Own what you did specifically and take responsibility for your actions or words. This step is very crucial. Admit that what you said was wrong and that it hurt your spouse. This will tell your spouse that you acknowledge the fact that you were wrong.

3. Show remorse for your actions. Let your spouse know that you feel horrible, terrible or sick at the thought of what you did or said. Express regret for your actions or words.

4. Reassure your partner how you are going to better behave the next time a similar situation arises in the future. Let your partner know that you are truly ready to repent and improve next time.

5. Ask if your spouse will forgive you and if he/she is not ready yet, give them some time. Find out if there is anything they will want you to do to better off the situation.

Let the goal of your apology be to repair the damage your actions or words caused and to restore your spouse's confidence and trust in you once more. Do not apologize for the sake of peace on something that you truly were the cause. Be intentional about improving subsequently and do not just mention mere words. May God help you as you seek to do the right thing.

HOW TO KEEP A HAPPY HOME

1). Never raise your voice for any reason to your husband. Its a sign of disrespect.

2). Don't expose your husband's weaknesses to your family and friends. It will bounce back at you.You are each other's keeper.

3). Never use attitudes and moods to communicate to your husband, you never know how your husband will interpret them. Defensive women don't have a happy home.

4). Never compare your husband to other men, you've no idea what their life is all about. If you attack his Ego, his Love for you will diminish.

5). Never ill treat your husband's friends because you don't like them, the person who's supposed to get rid of them is your husband.

6). Never forget that your husband married you, not your maid or anyone else. Do your duties.

7). Never assign anyone to give attention to your husband, people may do everything else but your husband is your own responsibility.

8). Never blame your husband if he comes back home empty handed. Rather encourage him.

9). Never be a wasteful wife, your husband's sweat is too precious to be wasted.

10). Never pretend to be sick for the purpose of denying your husband sex. You must give it to him how he wants it. Sex is very important to Men, if you keep denying him, it is a matter of time before another woman takes over your duty. No man can withstand sex starvation for too long(even the anointed ones)

11). Never compare your husband to your one time sex mate in bedroom, or an Ex-lover. Your home may Never recover from it if you do.

12). Never answer for your husband in public opinion polls, let him handle what is directed to him although he may answer for you in public opinion polls.

13). Never shout or challenge your husband in front of children. Wise Women don't do that.

14). Don't forget to check the smartness of your husband before he checks out.

15). Never allow your friends to be too close to your husband.

16). Never be in a hurry in the bathroom and on the dressing table. Out there your husband is always surrounded by women who took their time on their looks.

17). Your parents or family or friends do not have the final say in your marriage. Don't waste your time looking up to them for a final word. You must Leave if you want to Cleave.

18). Never base your love on monetary things. Will you still submit to him even if you earn more money than him?

19). Don't forget that husbands want attention and good listeners, never be too busy for him. Good communication is the bed rock of every happy home.

20). If your idea worked better than his, never compare yourself to him. Its always teamwork.

21). Don't be too judgemental to your husband. No man wants a Nagging wife.

22). A lazy wife is a careless wife. She doesn't even know that her body needs a bath.

23). Does your husband like a kind of cooked food?, try to change your cooking. No man jokes with food.

24). Never be too demanding to your husband,enjoy every moment, resource as it comes.

25). Make a glass of water the very first welcome to your husband and everyone entering your home. Sweetness of attitude is true beauty.

26). Don't associate with women who have a wrong mental attitude about marriage.

27). Your marriage is as valuable to you as the value that you give it. Recklessness is unacceptable.

28). Fruit of the womb is a blessing from the Lord, love your children and teach them well.

29). You are never too old to influence your home. Never reduce your care for your family for any reason.

30). A prayerful wife is a better equipped wife, pray always for your husband and family...

www.ingramcontent.com/pod-product-compliance
Lightning Source LLC
LaVergne TN
LVHW020533160826
845677LV00015B/4025

* 9 7 9 8 8 4 6 5 1 7 6 9 1 *